AMERICAN CIVIL WAR
World Conflict Series

• • • • • • • • • • • • • • • • • • •

Written by Deborah Thompson

GRADES 5 - 8
Reading Levels 3 - 4

Classroom Complete Press

P.O. Box 19729
San Diego, CA 92159
Tel: 1-800-663-3609 / Fax: 1-800-663-3608
Email: service@classroomcompletepress.com

www.classroomcompletepress.com

ISBN-13: 978-1-55319-355-5
ISBN-10: 1-55319-355-5

© 2007

Permission to Reproduce

Critical Thinking Skills

American Civil War

Skills For Critical Thinking	Background & Causes	Major Figures	Key Events	Major Battles	Human Meaning of the War	Effects & Outcomes
LEVEL 1 Knowledge						
• Recall Details		✓		✓		
• Match	✓	✓	✓	✓	✓	✓
• Sequence				✓		
• List				✓		
LEVEL 2 Comprehension						
• Compare Characters		✓				
• Summarize	✓			✓	✓	✓
• State Main Idea						✓
• Describe	✓		✓		✓	
• Interpret			✓			✓
LEVEL 3 Application						
• Choose Information	✓			✓		
• Identify Outcomes						✓
• Apply What is Learned		✓			✓	
• Make Connections	✓		✓	✓		
LEVEL 4 Analysis						
• Draw Conclusions		✓	✓			✓
• Infer Character Motivations		✓			✓	
• Identify Relationships	✓					
LEVEL 5 Synthesis						
• Predict		✓			✓	
• Design	✓	✓			✓	
• Create	✓		✓			✓
LEVEL 6 Evaluation						
• State and Defend an Opinion		✓		✓		
• Make Judgements		✓				
• Explain	✓	✓	✓	✓	✓	✓

Based on Bloom's Taxonomy

Contents

✔ **6 BONUS Activity Pages!** Additional worksheets for your students
✔ **6 BONUS Overhead Transparencies!** For use with your projection system
FREE!

- Go to our website: **www.classroomcompletepress.com/bonus**
- Enter item CC5500 – American Civil War
- Enter pass code CC5500D for Activity Pages. CC5500A for Overheads.

Assessment Rubric

American Civil War

Student's Name: _____ Assignment: _____ Level: _____

	Level 1	Level 2	Level 3	Level 4
Understanding Concepts	Demonstrates a limited understanding of concepts. Teacher assistance required	Demonstrates a basic understanding of concepts. Some teacher assistance required	Demonstrates a general understanding of concepts. Little teacher assistance required	Demonstrates a thorough understanding of concepts. Teacher assistance not required
Response to the Text	Expresses responses to the text with limited effectiveness, inconsistently supported with proof from the text	Expresses responses to the text with some effectiveness, supported with some proof from the text	Expresses responses to the text with considerable effectiveness, supported with appropriate proof from the text	Expresses responses to the text with a high degree of effectiveness, supported with concise and effective proof from the text
Interpretation, Application & Analysis	Interprets and applies concepts with limited effectiveness, with few, unrelated details and incorrect analysis	Interprets and applies concepts with some effectiveness, with some detail but with inconsistent analysis	Interprets and applies concepts with considerable effectiveness, with a variety of details; detailed analysis	Interprets and applies concepts with a high degree of effectiveness, with a variety of appropriate details and analysis

STRENGTHS:

WEAKNESSES:

NEXT STEPS:

Teacher Guide

Our resource has been created for ease of use by both TEACHERS and STUDENTS alike.

Introduction

This resource provides ready-to-use information and activities for remedial students in grades five to eight. Written to grade and using simplified language and vocabulary, social studies concepts are presented in a way that makes them more accessible to students and easier to understand. Comprised of reading passages, student activities and overhead transparencies, our resource can be used effectively for whole-class, small group and independent work.

How Is Our Resource Organized?

STUDENT HANDOUTS

Reading passages and **activities** (*in the form of reproducible worksheets*) make up the majority of our resource. The reading passages present important grade-appropriate information and concepts related to the topic. Embedded in each passage are one or more questions that ensure students understand what they have read.

For each reading passage there are BEFORE YOU READ activities and AFTER YOU READ activities.

- The BEFORE YOU READ activities prepare students for reading by setting a purpose for reading. They stimulate background knowledge and experience, and guide students to make connections between what they know and what they will learn. Important concepts and vocabulary are also presented.

- The AFTER YOU READ activities check students' comprehension of the concepts presented in the reading passage and extend their learning. Students are asked to give thoughtful consideration of the reading passage through creative and evaluative

short-answer questions, research, and extension activities.

The **Assessment Rubric** (*page 4*) is a useful tool for evaluating students' responses to many of the activities in our resource. The **Comprehension Quiz** (*page 37*) can be used for either a follow-up review or assessment at the completion of the unit.

PICTURE CUES

Our resource contains three main types of pages, each with a different purpose and use. A Picture Cue at the top of each page shows, at a glance, what the page is for.

🍎 **Teacher Guide**
- Information and tools for the teacher

✏️ **Student Handouts**
- Reproducible worksheets and activities

EZ✓ **Easy Marking™ Answer Key**
- Answers for student activities

EASY MARKING™ ANSWER KEY
Marking students' worksheets is fast and easy with this **Answer Key**. Answers are listed in columns – just line up the column with its corresponding worksheet, as shown, and see how every question matches up with its answer!

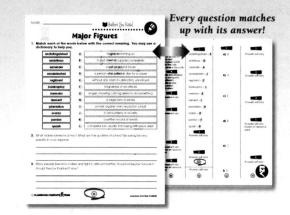

Every question matches up with its answer!

Bloom's Taxonomy

Our resource is an effective tool for any SOCIAL STUDIES PROGRAM.

Bloom's Taxonomy* for Reading Comprehension

The activities in our resource engage and build the full range of thinking skills that are essential for students' reading comprehension and understanding of important social studies concepts. Based on the six levels of thinking in Bloom's Taxonomy, and using language at a remedial level, information and questions are given that challenge students to not only recall what they have read, but move beyond this to understand the text and concepts through higher-order thinking. By using higher-order skills of application, analysis, synthesis and evaluation, students become active readers, drawing more meaning from the text, attaining a greater understanding of concepts, and applying and extending their learning in more sophisticated ways.

Our resource, therefore, is an effective tool for any Social Studies program. Whether it is used in whole or in part, or adapted to meet individual student needs, our resource provides teachers with essential information and questions to ask, inspiring students' interest, creativity, and promoting meaningful learning.

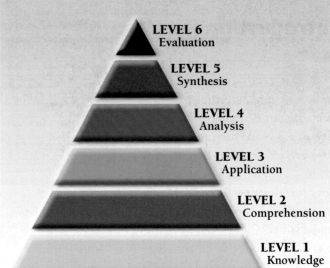

LEVEL 6
Evaluation

LEVEL 5
Synthesis

LEVEL 4
Analysis

LEVEL 3
Application

LEVEL 2
Comprehension

LEVEL 1
Knowledge

**BLOOM'S TAXONOMY:
6 LEVELS OF THINKING**

*Bloom's Taxonomy is a widely used tool by educators for classifying learning objectives, and is based on the work of Benjamin Bloom.

Vocabulary

seceded	legitimate	supersede	opposed	sections	resentment
depended	industrialized	illegal	valid	economy	abolitionism
undistinguished	ambitious	surrender	assassinated	regiment	bankruptcy
memoirs	demerits	plantation	martyr	pardon	quash
divided	materialized	determined	independent	sympathizer	controversial
overthrow	resolve	equality	barricaded	confidence	exhausted
retreated	private	casualties	priority	redefined	malnourished
unconditionally	dedication	impact	resourceful	strategies	homesick
discrimination	segregated	organization	manufacturing	menial	slavery
constitution	reconstruct	federal	goals	antebellum	amendments
dramatically	applied	watershed	legal	critical	

Background and Causes

1. **Put the correct vocabulary word on the line that matches the definition. You may use a dictionary to help you.**

seceded	legitimate	supersede
opposed	sections	resentment
depended	industrialized	illegal
valid	economy	abolitionism

_____ **a)** not allowed by the law

_____ **b)** well-founded; effective or legally binding

_____ **c)** to formally withdraw

_____ **d)** to rely on, especially for support or maintenance

_____ **e)** a distinct area; one of several pieces

_____ **f)** to introduce industry to an area

_____ **g)** the feeling of displeasure at something or someone

_____ **h)** the idea of wanting to end something, especially slavery

_____ **i)** to act against something; to stand in the way of something

_____ **j)** the way money and jobs are organized

_____ **k)** to take the place of something else

_____ **l)** according to the law; with well established rules

2. **The Civil War has been called one of the most important events in U.S. history. What do you already know about the Civil War? Create a list of names, dates, etc.**

_____

_____

_____

Background and Causes

T he American Civil War took place between 1861 and 1865 between the north and the south. The north included many states and had the backing of the federal government. The south was made up of eleven states that had **seceded**. The states that broke away were: South Carolina, Mississippi, Florida, Alabama, Georgia, Louisiana, Texas, Virginia, Arkansas, Tennessee and North Carolina.

> **The three main problems that led to the American Civil War were:**
> **slavery, industry in the north versus agriculture in the south, and states' rights.**

Beginning in 1840, the northern states **opposed** slavery. People in the south **depended** on slavery. Slaves were used on farms and plantations. Agriculture was the main industry in the south. The **economy** depended on slavery. People in the south were afraid of the anti-slavery ideas from the north. By the 1850s **abolitionism** was growing in the north. Abraham Lincoln, a strong anti-slavery Republican candidate, was elected president in 1860. At that point, the southern states seceded. They broke away from the north as a way to protect their way of life. The southern states were called the Confederate States of America and Jefferson Davis was their leader. President Lincoln said the Confederate States of America was not **valid** and that secession was **illegal**.

The northern states, also called the Northern States of the Federal Union, had more than two times the number of people living there than in the south. The north had highways, canals, and railroads. The north was **industrialized**, meaning that there were factories and more sophisticated jobs. Due to this, more immigrants were coming to the north, especially from Europe. As well, since the rest of the world saw the United States as a **legitimate** country, the north was able to continue trading with other countries. The south depended on agriculture and farming. There were not the same opportunities in the south as there were in the north. This also led to feelings of **resentment**. Further, since there were more people living in the north than in the south, the north had more representatives in the government. This continued to make the people in the south feel threatened. They were afraid that they would have no power.

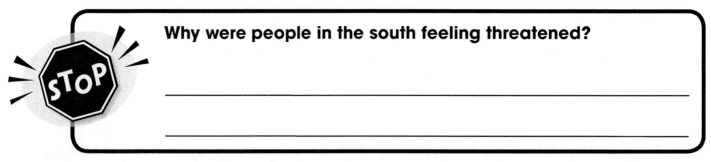

Why were people in the south feeling threatened?

_____

_____

States in the north were becoming very powerful because they had large numbers of people living there. Southern states had fewer people and therefore, less power. People began to talk about the country in terms of **sections**, or parts. This was called sectionalism. The south did not want to be controlled by the federal government. They believed that the laws of each individual state should be more important than federal laws. This became known as "states' rights". The south wanted the state laws to **supersede** any federal laws. States' rights became an important issue during the war.

After You Read 📖

Background and Causes

1. **Circle** the word True if the statement is true. **Circle** the word False if it is false.

a) There were more people living in the north than in the south.
   True   False

b) People in the south felt very powerful.
   True   False

c) The north depended on agriculture.
   True   False

d) Abraham Lincoln was elected President in 1860.
   True   False

e) Eleven southern states seceded.
   True   False

f) Northern states did not oppose slavery.
   True   False

g) Jefferson Davis became the leader of the Confederate States.
   True   False

h) The south wanted the federal laws to supersede the state laws.
   True   False

2. Use the words in the box to answer each question.

abolitionism	illegal	resentment	supersede
opposed	valid	industrialized	economy
sections	legitimate	depended	seceded

The Civil War took place between the northern states and the southern states that had

_____. President Lincoln, who _____ slavery did not see the southern
  a   **b**

states as being _____ or _____. He said the secession was _____.
                      c   **d**   **e**

_____ was becoming popular in the north, where the _____ was more
   f   **g**

_____ than the south, where the economy _____ on agriculture. There
   h   **i**

was growing _____ in the south, especially as people started talking about the
                    j

country in _____. States' rights became an important issue as the southern states
                 k

believed that state law should _____ any federal law. This was important to the
                                        l

south where the population was much smaller than the north.

Background and Causes

3. Explain why people in the south depended on slavery.

_____

_____

4. What were some of the major differences between the northern states and the southern states?

_____

_____

5. President Lincoln wanted to abolish slavery. Is there any law or practice occurring now that you think the president should abolish? Explain your answer.

_____

_____

Research & Application

6. The Civil War is one of the most important events in American history. **Interview three different people** from three different age groups (a friend, a parent, etc.). Find out what they know about the war. Below are some questions you could ask. Record the answers so that you can share your findings with the class.

> • When was the Civil War? • How did you learn about it? • Who was involved?
> • Who won? • What were the major issues? • What changed in the end?
> • What do you want to know about the Civil War?

7. The word "**abolitionism**" can be hard to understand. Do some more research to find out what the word means. What is the root word? How can the word be used? **Create a poster** to show what the word means and how it can be used. Be ready to share your poster with the class.

8. Many countries allowed slavery for many years. Do some research to find out the **origins of slavery**. When and where did it start? Why did slavery occur? What was the purpose? Who was involved? Create a display to show your research results. Decide with your teacher if you will create a poster, pamphlet, PowerPoint presentation, backboard display, essay, etc. Choose a presentation method that you have not tried before.

NAME: _____

Major Figures

1. Match each of the words below with the correct meaning. You may use a dictionary to help you.

undistinguished	A	to give something up
ambitious	B	to put down or suppress completely
surrender	C	a unit of ground forces
assassinated	D	a person who suffers or dies for a cause
regiment	E	without any claim to distinction; unnoticed
bankruptcy	F	forgiveness of an offense
memoirs	G	eager; showing a strong desire to do something
demerit	H	a large farm or estate
plantation	I	a mark against one's record for a fault
martyr	J	to kill suddenly or secretly
pardon	K	a written record of events
quash	L	complete ruin, usually from being in massive debt

2. What makes someone a hero? What are the qualities of a hero? Be sure to be very specific in your response.

_____

_____

_____

3. Many people become soldiers and fight in different battles. Should soldiers be honored? Should they be thanked? How?

_____

_____

_____

Reading Passage

NAME: _____

Major Figures

There were many important people in the Civil War. Below are some of the individuals who were considered to be the major figures in the Civil War.

Abraham Lincoln was born in Kentucky on February 12, 1809. Although he came from an **undistinguished** family, Lincoln worked hard to receive an education. He was extremely **ambitious** and received a law degree. He married Mary Todd and had four children, although only one survived to be an adult.

He ran for Senator in 1858 but lost to a man named Stephen A. Douglas. Even though he lost, he gained national recognition for his ability to speak in public. In 1860 he became President. He worked hard and built up the Republican Party. On January 1, 1863 he issued his famous Emancipation Proclamation.

In 1864 Lincoln won re-election. With the end of the war near, he encouraged those fighting in the south to **surrender.** He worked to promote peace. On Friday, April 14, 1865 Abraham Lincoln was **assassinated**. He is remembered as being a kind person.

During the Civil War, **Ulysses S. Grant** was the General of the Union army. He was born in 1822 to a family from Ohio. As a young man, Grant attended West Point even though he did not really want to attend school. When the Civil War started, Grant was working in Illinois at his family's leather store. He became the leader of a volunteer **regiment** and got the regiment ready for service. Within a year, Grant became Brigadier General of the volunteers. In February 1862 President Lincoln promoted Grant to Major General of volunteers. Two years later, due to his strong ability to fight and lead, he was appointed General-in-Chief.

Grant fought against many Confederate forces including General Robert E. Lee who surrendered to Grant in 1865. Grant became President of the United States in 1868. He was considered an obvious choice for president after his many accomplishments during the Civil War. After his presidency, Grant was a partner in a financial business that lasted only a short time before declaring **bankruptcy**. Shortly thereafter Grant learned that he had cancer of the throat. Dying, and knowing that he had nothing to leave his family, Grant frantically started writing his **memoirs** which earned him a great deal of money. He died in 1885, not long after he completed his book.

Reading Passage

• •

Major Figures

Jefferson Davis was born on June 3, 1808 and grew up in Mississippi. He had a tough childhood as the youngest of ten children. After going to Transylvania University, Davis went to West Point and graduated with more than 327 **demerits** on his record.

In 1835 Davis married but his wife died only three months later. Wanting to start a new life, Davis moved to Mississippi to be near his brother. He worked on a **plantation** for almost ten years before marrying again in 1845. In 1846 he became commander of a volunteer group called the 1st Mississippi Rifles. In 1847 he became a senator but resigned in 1851 to run for governor. He went back to being a senator from 1853 to 1857. He often spoke in favor of slavery and states' rights.

Davis became President of the Confederate States in 1861 even though he was not a strong leader. He often focused on military activities and ignored everything else. He also hired close friends for jobs that they were incapable of doing.

In 1865 as the Confederacy was falling apart, Davis fled from Virginia. He wanted to keep fighting and form a new government. On May 10th 1865, Davis was captured in Georgia. He was put in prison for two years and soon was seen as a **martyr**. Davis was never brought to trial and was released in 1867. Refusing to get a **pardon**, Davis moved to Mississippi where he spent time writing. He died on December 6, 1889.

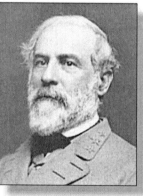

Robert E. Lee was born on January 19, 1807. He was the fourth son and was raised mainly by his mother. Robert's father was not a strong provider, and Robert learned to work hard in life to ensure that he did succeed. He attended the U.S. Military Academy and graduated with no demerits; a record that to this day has not been matched. Upon graduation, Lee worked as an engineer in St. Louis. He also married Mary Custis, the granddaughter of George Washington.

When the southern states seceded, Lee was asked to take command of the U.S. Army to **quash** the rebellion. Instead of accepting, Lee offered his services to Jefferson Davis who has just been elected President of the Confederate States of America. Lee led numerous attacks. He was very bold and developed good strategies for war. The biggest battle was fought at Gettysburg, Pennsylvania in July 1863. Lee continued to fight until he surrendered at Appomattox Court House on April 9, 1865. This is generally seen as the end of the Civil War. After the war, Lee became President of Washington University, where he stayed until his death in 1870.

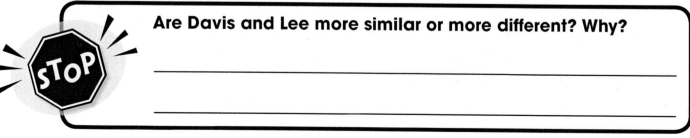

Are Davis and Lee more similar or more different? Why?

_____

_____

NAME: _____

Major Figures

1. **The following are multiple choice questions. Circle the correct answer.**

   a) **Abraham Lincoln was:**
      - A from a poor family
      - B ambitious
      - C smart
      - D not very tall

   b) **Ulysses S. Grant was the:**
      - A General of the Union Army
      - B best soldier in the war
      - C youngest of fourteen children
      - D Commander of the Confederate Forces

   c) **Jefferson Davis:**
      - A worked on a plantation for ten years
      - B became president of the Confederate States of America
      - C graduated with more than 327 demerits on his record
      - D was captured in Georgia
      - E all of the above

   d) **Robert E. Lee:**
      - A was raised mainly by his father
      - B has a demerit record that has not been matched
      - C worked as an engineer in Chicago
      - D became President of the United States
      - E none of the above

   e) **Who was never President of the United States?**
      - A Abraham Lincoln
      - B Ulysses S. Grant
      - C Robert E. Lee
      - D All of the above
      - E None of the above

   f) **Who was regarded as a martyr for the cause?**
      - A Robert E. Lee
      - B Abraham Lincoln
      - C Ulysses S. Grant
      - D Jefferson Davis

After You Read

Major Figures

2. Robert E. Lee was asked to take command of the U.S. Army. Instead, he offered his services to Davis and the Confederate forces. Why do you think he did this?

_____

_____

3. As a child and a student, **Abraham Lincoln** was called "ambitious". Later in life he experienced great success, even becoming President. Do you think that everyone who is ambitious is also successful? Explain your answer fully.

_____

_____

4. Memoirs are written by people who observed events or participated in various events. Do you think memoirs should be considered fact? Should memoirs be read as novels and be considered more like fiction? Explain your answer.

_____

_____

Research & Application

5. Plantations were located all over the United States, especially in the southern states. Do some research to find out:

> • What a plantation was • What it looked like • Who worked there
> • Who owned them • What life was like on a plantation

Then **create a poster** to show what you found out. If you wish, create an **aerial view** of the plantation for your poster. Be ready to put your poster up in your classroom and share your ideas with your classmates.

6. Imagine that Abraham Lincoln, Ulysses S. Grant, Jefferson Davis and Robert E. Lee are all in the same room together. What would their conversation sound like? What would they say to each other? **Create a dialogue script** between the four men. Write down what each of the men say to each other. Be sure that each "character" has **at least six** lines. Once your script is written, get a group together to read the script and act out the scene.

Key Events of the Civil War

1. **Match each of the words below with the correct meaning. You may use a dictionary to help you.**

divided	A	a person who shares the same feelings, concerns or ideas
materialized	B	the ability to be equal with something or someone else
determined	C	separated into parts
independent	D	a resolution, decision or promise to do something
sympathizer	E	to come into being; to happen; to take place
controversial	F	decided, settled, resolved
overthrow	G	not influenced or controlled by anyone
resolve	H	to overcome or defeat; to put an end to something
equality	I	something debatable, questionable, not easily agreed upon

2. Many people have determination to do something or to accomplish something. What are you determined about? How do you show determination?

_____

_____

3. In the Civil War people were willing to fight for what they believed in. Both sides believed so strongly in their own ideas that they went to war. Can you think of something that you believe in strongly? What would you be willing to fight for?

_____

_____

4. Sometimes ideas can be controversial, meaning that not everyone agrees with them. What are some controversial ideas facing your family, school, community, or country?

_____

_____

NAME: _____

Key Events of the Civil War

After Abraham Lincoln was elected President in 1860, some southern states seceded from the Union. The main issue was slavery. People in the south depended on slaves to work on the farms and plantations. Northerners believed that if slaves were free, they could then work in the factories. The north and the south were **divided**.

Jefferson Davis became President of the Confederate States of America. He believed in protecting slave owners and maintaining the way of life in the south. Davis and his supporters developed an army who were willing to fight for what they believed in.

Davis' forces attacked Fort Sumter, South Carolina on April 12, 1861. This was the beginning of the Civil War. The attack lasted many hours and the fort was severely damaged. Amazingly, no one was killed in the attack. Fort Sumter fell to the Confederate commanders. President Lincoln, who had worked very hard to try and avoid war, called for volunteers to become involved. People were surprised by this call.

Many people believed that the war would not last long. They expected fighting to last only a few weeks. No one recognized how **determined** the south was to become **independent**, and how determined the north was to end the rebellion from the south.

On January 1, 1863 President Lincoln issued the Emancipation Proclamation. This was an executive order giving freedom to all slaves. The proclamation was **controversial.** Since it was an executive order, President Lincoln did not need it passed by Congress. The freedom was meant not only for slaves in states under Union control, but also for those slaves living in the Confederate States of America. The proclamation only furthered the **resolve** of people in the south to keep fighting. Both Britain and France supported the Emancipation Proclamation. Lincoln's order had support from other countries at a time when it was greatly needed. This strengthened the north even more.

November 19, 1863 was another turning point in the Civil War. President Lincoln delivered the Gettysburg Address. Standing at the Soldier's National Cemetery in Gettysburg, Pennsylvania, President Lincoln stirred up the emotions of all people. His speech was quite short: fewer than 300 words and under three minutes in length. He said that the Civil War was meant to preserve the government "of the people, by the people, and for the people". He said that the war was not just a battle for the Union, but that it would bring freedom and **equality** to everyone living in the United States.

One of the last major events in the Civil War was the assassination, or killing, of President Lincoln. He was shot on April 14, 1865 by John Wilkes Booth. On the same day, the Secretary of State, William H. Seward was attacked by Lewis Powell. Both of the men who attacked Lincoln and Seward were Confederate **sympathizers**. Booth and Powell believed that if they killed both the President and the Secretary of State, they could **overthrow** the federal government. There was even an attack planned on the Vice-President, but those plans never **materialized**.

After You Read

Key Events of the Civil War

1. Below are two columns. Column A has the beginning of a sentence. Column B has the ending of a sentence. Match up Column A and Column B to make **ten true statements**. Go back to the reading to check your answers.

	Column A		Column B
a	One of the last major events in the Civil War	A	had an immediate impact on slaves and the military
b	President Lincoln	B	called themselves the Confederate States of America
c	Britain and France	C	delivered the Gettysburg Address on November 19, 1863
d	Many people	D	stirred up the emotions of people living in the north and in the south
e	The seceded states	E	supported the Emancipation Proclamation
f	Fort Sumter	F	was the assassination of President Lincoln
g	President Lincoln	G	does not need to be passed by Congress
h	The Emancipation Proclamation	H	signaled the beginning of the Civil War
i	An executive order	I	was attacked by Confederate Forces on April 12, 1861
j	The attack on Fort Sumter	J	believed that the war would not last long

2. Do you think that the assassination of President Lincoln led to the end of the Civil War, or do you think the war would have ended when it did even if the President survived?

_____

_____

_____

_____

Key Events of the Civil War

3. **Use the words in the box below to fill in the blanks. Go back to the reading passage to check your answers.**

equality	resolve	overthrow
controversial	sympathizers	independent
determined	materialized	divided

_____ a) Booth and Powell were called these

_____ b) Lincoln said everyone would have this

_____ c) The Emancipation Proclamation was called this

_____ d) The north and south were not together

_____ e) The south wanted to be out on their own

_____ f) Plans to take over the government did not happen

_____ g) Name given to south; they did not give up

_____ h) A promise or decision

_____ i) Booth and Powell wanted to do this

Research & Application

4. The **Gettysburg Address** has been called one of the most popular and important speeches in American history. Despite that, the exact wording of the speech has been disputed. There are five different manuscripts, or copies, of the Gettysburg Address. Do some research to find **at least three** of them. Read the speech (it is less than 300 words) and then find out what the differences are. Include the source information from where you read the speech. **Create a chart** similar to the one below to show what you have discovered.

Differences in the Gettysburg Address

Speech #1	Speech #2	Speech #3
Source:	Source:	Source:

NAME: _____

Major Battles

1. **Write the word on the line that matches the definition. Use a dictionary to help you.**

barricaded	surrendered	confidence
exhausted	retreated	private
casualties	priority	redefined
malnourished	unconditionally	dedication

_____ **a)** a soldier of low rank

_____ **b)** going back or withdrawing

_____ **c)** to shut in, or obstruct

_____ **d)** not having the right food or enough food

_____ **e)** having a high order of importance

_____ **f)** people who are injured or killed, especially in a war

_____ **g)** giving a new meaning to something

_____ **h)** to give up or to give back

_____ **i)** to wear out completely; to be completely tired

_____ **j)** not limited by anything; something that is absolute

_____ **k)** belief in the powers and abilities of oneself or another

_____ **l)** a ceremony marking the opening or start of something

2. **Have you ever had an argument with someone? What did you argue or fight about? How did the argument start? How did it end?**

_____

_____

_____

_____

Major Battles

Attack on Fort Sumter - April 12, 1861

When Fort Sumter was fired on, it was considered the beginning of the U.S. Civil War. The fort was located near Charleston, South Carolina, a seceded state. The southern states wanted to take over the fort, but the federal government did not want to give it up. The commander locked himself and his troops inside the fort while waiting for help. When the **barricaded** troops ran out of food, southern forces attacked the fort for 36 hours. In the end, the fort **surrendered**. No one was killed in the attack.

First Battle of Bull Run - July 21, 1861 & Second Battle of Bull Run – August 28-30, 1862

These battles were also called "Manassas". General McDowell led the Union forces and General Beauregard and General Johnston led the Confederate forces in the first battle. This was the first major land battle of the Civil War. It took place southwest of Washington, D.C. In the first battle, people from the city came to the battlefield to watch. Little did they know that it would be a bloody and brutal battle. At first the Confederates were losing the battle, until they noticed the crowds watching them. The Confederates gained **confidence** and fought harder. The Confederates beat the Union forces but were too **exhausted** to chase the Union forces away. They **retreated** without being completely wiped out. The second battle was also a victory for the southern forces.

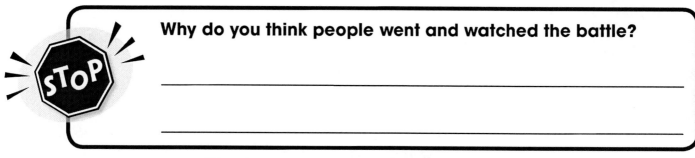

Why do you think people went and watched the battle?

_____

_____

Monitor vs. Merrimac – March 8, 1862

This was also called the Battle of Hampton Roads. This was a naval battle, meaning that it took place at sea. The Monitor was a Union forces ship and the Merrimac was a Confederate forces ship. Later, the Merrimac was renamed the "Virginia". Both battleships were extremely powerful and the battle was evenly matched. The battle was ended as a draw. This means that neither side won. In the end the Merrimac retreated.

The Battle of Antietam – September 17, 1862

This was also called the Battle of Sharpsburg. It was the first major battle to take place on Northern territory. After winning at Manassas, Lee was feeling confident. He moved towards Maryland, but a Union **private** found a copy of Lee's battle plans. Despite this advantage, the northern forces did not do as well as expected. Although some historians say the battle was a draw, others say it was a victory for the North. This was the bloodiest and most deadly single battle of the war. It was also the bloodiest single-day battle in American history with almost 23,000 **casualties**.

NAME: _____

Major Battles

The Battle of Fredericksburg – December 13, 1862

This battle took place in Virginia. The battle was between General Lee's Confederate Army and Major General Ambrose Burnside's Union Army. The Battle of Fredericksburg was a big victory for the south. It is remembered as being one of the most one-sided battles in the Civil War. The Union Army suffered many casualties.

We get the name "sideburns" for long facial hair from Major General Burnside.

Battle of Vicksburg – Spring 1863

It was a **priority** for the Union Army to gain control of the Mississippi River. Vicksburg, Mississippi was one of the last cities along the river that was not under Union control. Grant was given the job of ensuring that Vicksburg fell from the Confederate forces. It was a very difficult battle. The Union troops made several attempts to take over the city, but each one failed. Finally, the Union troops surrounded Vicksburg, blocking all shipments of food and supplies from entering the city. Citizens and soldiers held out as long as they could. On July 4, 1863 Vicksburg surrendered to the Union Army.

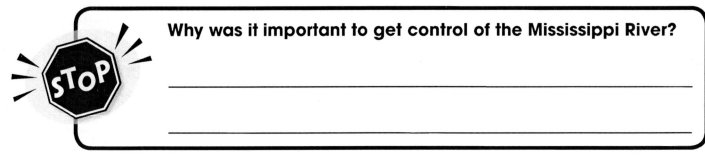

Why was it important to get control of the Mississippi River?

_____

_____

Battle of Gettysburg – July 1-3, 1863

The Battle of Gettysburg is often referred to as the "turning point" of the war. Lee moved his army into Pennsylvania and unexpectedly met the Union army. The battle was extremely bloody, with close to 50,000 casualties. The battle was a major victory for the Union forces, as it kept the southern forces from moving northward. In November 1863, Lincoln gave the Gettysburg Address at the **dedication** ceremony for the Gettysburg National Cemetery. In that speech, Lincoln **redefined** the purpose of the war.

Battle of Appomattox Court House – April 9, 1865

General Lee was becoming desperate. Ulysses S. Grant's troops had broken through Lee's defenses, and forced the Confederates to retreat. As they moved back they burned their capital city of Richmond. They did this so that the city would be useless to the Union Army. Lee's troops were exhausted and **malnourished**. Lee needed to escape the Union Army who was closing in on him. At dawn on April 9, 1865, Union troops formed a line of battle at Appomattox Court House and then surrounded the Confederates. With nowhere to turn, Lee **unconditionally** surrendered to Grant at the Appomattox Court House in Virginia. After agreeing to the surrender, Grant gave Lee's soldiers food and water. Although there was still some fighting after the surrender, April 9, 1865 is considered the end of the war.

Major Battles

1. **Below is a list of events that took place during the Civil War. Put the events in the order in which they occurred. Place a 1 on the line for the first event, a 2 for the second event, and so forth. Go back to the reading to check your answers.**

_____ **a)** On July 4, 1863 Vicksburg surrendered to the Union Army.

_____ **b)** The first major land battle of the Civil War takes place.

_____ **c)** A Union private found a copy of Lee's battle plans.

_____ **d)** The Confederates beat the Union forces but were too exhausted to chase them away.

_____ **e)** It was a priority for the Union Army to gain control of the Mississippi River.

_____ **f)** Fort Sumter was fired on.

_____ **g)** Union troops formed a line of battle at Appomattox Court House.

_____ **h)** Lee moved his army into Pennsylvania and unexpectedly met the Union army.

_____ **i)** A naval battle took place, called the Battle of Hampton Roads.

_____ **j)** Grant was given the job of ensuring that Vicksburg fell from the Confederates.

_____ **k)** Lee unconditionally surrendered to Grant.

_____ **l)** The first major battle of the war to take place on Northern territory was fought.

_____ **m)** The Union Army suffered many casualties in the Battle of Fredericksburg.

_____ **n)** The Merrimac retreated.

_____ **o)** President Lincoln gave the Gettysburg Address.

2. In your own words explain what a naval battle is.

_____

_____

3. Why do you think the Battle of Gettysburg is called a "turning point" in the war?

_____

_____

Major Battles

4. Lincoln gave the Gettysburg Address at the dedication ceremony for the cemetery. Think of **at least three** other "dedications" in history.

_____

_____

5. The words **redefined**, **malnourished**, and **unconditionally** have prefixes and suffixes. A prefix is something that is added to the beginning of a word, and a suffix is something that is added to the end of a word. Without prefixes or suffixes, the word is called a "root word". Complete the chart below to find out the root word, the prefix and suffix.

	redefined	malnourished	Unconditionally
Prefix			
Suffix			
Root Word			

Research & Application

6. Many towns and cities across America have monuments, statues and memorials relating to the Civil War. In other towns, buildings such as schools and arenas are named after Civil War heroes. Find out if there is a building or monument in your community. Go and visit it. Try to find out **at least ten** different things about it. Listed below are some ideas that you can use:

Name of place	**Inscriptions**	**Community involvement**
Type of place	**Date of construction**	**Date of dedication**
Location	**Size**	**Three other facts**

7. During the Civil War, General Lee's war plans were found by a private. A private is a low ranking officer. Do some research to find out the **different ranks** in the U.S. military. **Create a poster or pamphlet** to show what you have learned.

8. There were many battles in the Civil War. Investigate **three other battles** not mentioned in this section. Try to use a variety of different resources.

	Battle #1	Battle #2	Battle #3
Name of Battle			
Place			
Important Leaders			
Events leading to battle			
Winners/Losers			
Major outcomes			
Casualties			

The Human Meaning of the War

1. **Write the word on the line that matches the definition. Use a dictionary to help you.**

impact	resourceful	strategies
homesick	discrimination	segregated
organization	manufacturing	menial

_____ **a)** to have an influence or an effect

_____ **b)** lowly and sometimes degrading

_____ **c)** treatment against someone

_____ **d)** able to deal skillfully, especially when faced with new situations

_____ **e)** feeling sad or depressed when away from home or family

_____ **f)** to separate from others or from a group

_____ **g)** plans or methods to reach a goal

_____ **h)** system or structure

_____ **i)** the making of goods

2. Have you ever been away from your family or friends for a long period of time? Where did you go? How did you feel? Were you happy to return? Explain.

_____

_____

3. Think of a time when you were left out of a group. It may be been done on purpose or by accident. How did you feel?

_____

_____

4. What is a goal that you want to reach? How do you go about reaching that goal?

_____

_____

The Human Meaning of the War

The Civil War had a huge **impact** on many people's lives. Many people were involved in the war. There were generals, soldiers and volunteers involved directly in the fighting. There were family members who saw their loved ones leave to go and fight. The war also had an impact on slaves, freed slaves, and women.

Many of the men who joined the army had never been away from home. They became **homesick**. To overcome their homesickness, soldiers kept in touch with their family by writing letters. Each day, almost 90,000 letters passed through Washington, D.C.

Both the Confederate and Union armies lacked **organization**. The soldiers did not get enough training, food or clothing. Even though their lives were difficult, soldiers in the Civil War tended to be young, upbeat, and **resourceful**.

When soldiers were not fighting or drilling techniques and strategies, many of them were bored. Soldiers spent time making meals, cutting firewood, and writing letters. Gambling and games such as dominoes helped to pass the time between making **strategies** and fighting in battles. Often soldiers would sit around a campfire at night telling stories from home and singing songs.

Does sharing stories make one feel more or less homesick? Explain.

_____

_____

Black soldiers played an important role in the Civil War. They were allowed to enlist in the Union Army. The Confederate Army used slaves as crew members on their ships. Black soldiers were usually paid less than white soldiers, had **menial** jobs, and faced a great deal of **discrimination**. They often fought in **segregated** groups with a white officer as their commander.

At home, the Civil War divided families and friends. People who were neighbors and friends were on opposite sides of the war. Much of the war took place in the south, and major cities such as Atlanta and Richmond were destroyed. Disease spread among towns and villages and many people died. As men went off to war, women were left to look after children, run businesses and maintain farms throughout the country.

Women worked together and formed various groups such as the Soldier's Aid Society. In the north and the south, women's groups made bandages for wounded soldiers. Women sewed clothing and knit socks and garments. Some women also volunteered to work as nurses to care for the wounded. Women worked in **manufacturing** as well and helped make ammunition, uniforms and other supplies for the soldiers.

Louisa May Alcott, author of <u>Little Women</u>, worked as a nurse during the war.

NAME: _____

After You Read

The Human Meaning of the War

1. **Circle** the word True if the statement is true. **Circle** the word False if it is false.

   a) Black soldiers played an important part in the Civil War.
   True   **False**

   b) The Confederate forces were well organized.
   True   **False**

   c) Most of the fighting in the Civil War took place in the north.
   True   **False**

   d) Soldiers were homesick.
   True   **False**

   e) Women sewed clothes for soldiers.
   True   **False**

   f) Some women volunteered as nurses during the Civil War.
   True   **False**

   g) Black soldiers were treated the same as white soldiers.
   True   **False**

   h) Many of the soldiers in the Civil War were resourceful.
   True   **False**

   i) Soldiers hardly ever wrote letters home.
   True   **False**

   j) While men were away, women looked after farms and businesses.
   True   **False**

2. Explain how people who were friends before the war could turn into enemies during the Civil War.

   _____

   _____

3. Does discrimination exist today? Explain your ideas. Try to think about your community, your country, and the world.

   _____

   _____

4. The Civil War had a huge impact on many people. What are some events that have had a huge impact on your life? Explain your response.

   _____

   _____

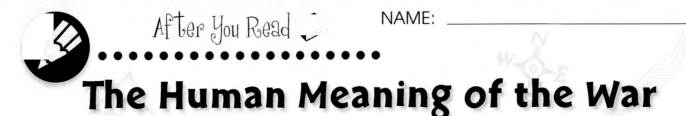
The Human Meaning of the War

5. Use the words in the box to fill in the blanks below.

segregated	resourceful	strategies
organization	homesick	discrimination
manufacturing	impact	menial

The Civil War had an _____ on many people. Many soldiers
         a

left home to fight. The armies lacked _____, and the soldiers were often
           b

_____ . Despite this, soldiers were very _____ and
    c   **d**

adapted to their situation. They often wrote letters home when they were not

practicing _____ for battle. Black soldiers also played an important
         e

role in the Civil War. Often these soldiers experienced _____. They were
                f

_____ and put into different groups. They were given _____
    g   **h**

jobs to do. While the men were away, women took care of the children, farms, and

businesses. Some women also worked in _____ to make things the soldiers
         i

needed.

Research & Application

6. Many women were involved in the Civil War. Do some research on **one** of the women
listed below. Use the chart on the next page to help you organize your information.

Important Women of the Civil War

- Rose O'Neal Greenhow
- Clara Barton
- Harriet Beecher Stowe
- Mary Todd Lincoln
- Mary Edwards Walker

- Varnia Jefferson Davis
- Pauline Cushman
- Dorothea Lynde Dix
- Sarah Emma Edmonds
- Elizabeth Cady Stanton

7. You have read a little bit about the life of a soldier during the Civil War. Do some research
to find out more about the life of a soldier. **Investigate the life of a soldier.** Write **two
journal entries**, one from the viewpoint of a white soldier, and one from the viewpoint of
a black soldier. Be ready to share your journal entries with the class.

Important Women of the Civil War

Name	
Place and Date of Birth	
Family Background	
Education	
Hometown	
Details of Daily Life	
Importance in the Civil War	
Place and Date of Death	
At least three other points	

NAME: _____

Effects and Outcomes

1. Match each of the words below with the correct meaning. You may use a dictionary to help you.

slavery	A	the purpose of doing something
constitution	B	the time before the Civil War
reconstruct	C	an event that shows an important time of change in history
federal	D	something that is lawful or is allowed by the law
goals	E	putting someone under the control of another person
antebellum	F	changes or additions
amendments	G	relating to the entire country
dramatically	H	the basic beliefs and laws of a country
applied	I	important or vital
watershed	J	to build again
legal	K	suddenly or surprisingly; obviously different
critical	L	put into use

2. Think of a time in your life when you were able to do something, or allowed to do something (i.e., you join a new sports team because you reached the right age). How did other people treat you as a newcomer? How did you want to be treated?

_____

_____

_____

3. If someone asked you to explain what the constitution is, what would you say?

_____

_____

_____

Effects and Outcomes

T he Civil War ended when General Robert E. Lee surrendered at the Appomattox Court House. The surrender took place on April 9, 1865. Even though the war was officially over in the Spring of 1865, many important things happened after the war.

Much of the fighting during the war took place in the south. President Lincoln had a plan to **reconstruct** the south. He wanted to fix the damage. He wanted to reorganize the union to include the southern states, especially the states that had seceded. When Lincoln was killed in April 1865, many of his reconstruction plans died with him.

Winning the war meant more than just ending the battles. Northern leaders had two main **goals**. They wanted to be sure that the southern states would return to the Union and end their ideas of secession. They also wanted **slavery** to end. The problem was that the leaders could not agree on how these two goals should be met.

The **federal** government made some very important changes. Three **amendments**, or changes, were made to the U.S. **Constitution**.

> **13th Amendment: Slavery shall no longer exist in the United States.**
> **14th Amendment: All citizens of the United States are entitled to be treated equally and fairly, and to have their legal rights respected.**
> **15th Amendment: All citizens of the United States have the right to vote.**

The Civil War has been called a **watershed** event in the U.S. This means that the Civil War was an event that signaled **critical** change. There were many important changes following the war. After years of war and terrible destruction, the individual states became a much stronger union. No individual state ever seceded again, and states' rights were no longer discussed. More importantly, the Civil War put an end to slavery.

Life in the U.S. changed greatly after the Civil War. For people in the south, their way of life changed **dramatically**. They had a specific, or **antebellum**, way of life. Slavery was a very big part of that. Slaves lived and worked together on farms and plantations. When slavery was no longer **legal**, people had to change their way of life as well as their attitudes. After the war, slaves were free men and women. The constitution and all the amendments **applied** to them. It took a long time for freed slaves to be accepted. Though the war ended slavery, racism and discrimination continued to exist, even today.

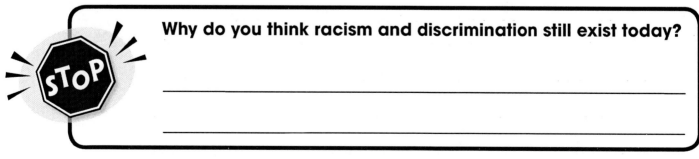

Why do you think racism and discrimination still exist today?

_____

_____

Effects and Outcomes

1. **The following are multiple choice questions. Circle the correct answer.**

   a) **When did the Civil War end?**

   A   Once the fighting stopped

   B   April 9, 1865

   C   When General Robert E. Lee died

   D   As soon as the troops met at the Appomattox Court House

   E   None of the above

   b) **What was the antebellum way of life?**

   A   Work as hard as you can

   B   Sleep until noon and work until sunset

   C   Keep slaves to work on farms and plantations

   D   People work and live together in the same house

   c) **This was the number of changes the government made to the constitution after the Civil War.**

   A   13th, 14th and 15th

   B   four

   C   none

   D   three

   d) **This was President Lincoln's plan.**

   A   Reconstruction

   B   Re-settlement

   C   Damage control

   D   All of the above

   e) **Northern leaders wanted this:**

   A   Southern states to be punished

   B   Southern states to remain seceded

   C   Southern states to rejoin the union

   D   All of the above

   E   None of the above

   f) **Another goal that northern leaders had was to:**

   A   Shut down all plantations

   B   Abolish slavery

   C   Send everyone to school

   D   None of the above

NAME: _____

After You Read 📖

Effects and Outcomes

2. Use the words in the box to fill in the blanks below.

slavery	constitution	reconstruct	watershed
dramatically	critical	legal	amendments

The Civil War has been called a _____ event in American history. Many changes
a
took place after the war ended. President Lincoln wanted to _____ the south.
b
Several changes were made to the _____. These changes were called_____.
c **d**
One of the _____, or important changes involved _____. The constitution
e **f**
abolished slavery; it was no longer _____. This _____ changed the way of life
g **h**
for many people, especially those who lived in the south.

3. What were the major changes that took place after the Civil War?

_____

_____

4. Explain why the Civil War is one of the most important events in American history.

_____

_____

Research & Application

5. Since the Civil War there have been a number of **amendments** made to the U.S. constitution. Do some research and read about the amendments. Choose **three** that you think are important or interesting. **Create a three-panel poster or pamphlet** to highlight these amendments. Include a short summary, important dates, and how the amendments apply to you. Be ready to share your work.

6. a) The Constitution is a set of rules that explains how people should live. If you had to create a constitution for your classroom, what kind of rules would you include? Using the graphic organizer on the next page, brainstorm some ideas for your own classroom constitution. Remember, the rules that you create apply to you too!

   b) Once you have created your list, write a short two to three minute speech telling the class what your constitution is about. Practice your speech before you give it.

   c) If time permits, have a vote in your classroom to pick one of the constitutions. Try to choose one that you think would be good for everyone in your class. Throughout the year reflect on the constitution and see if you need to make any "amendments" to it.

NAME: _____

Classroom Constitution

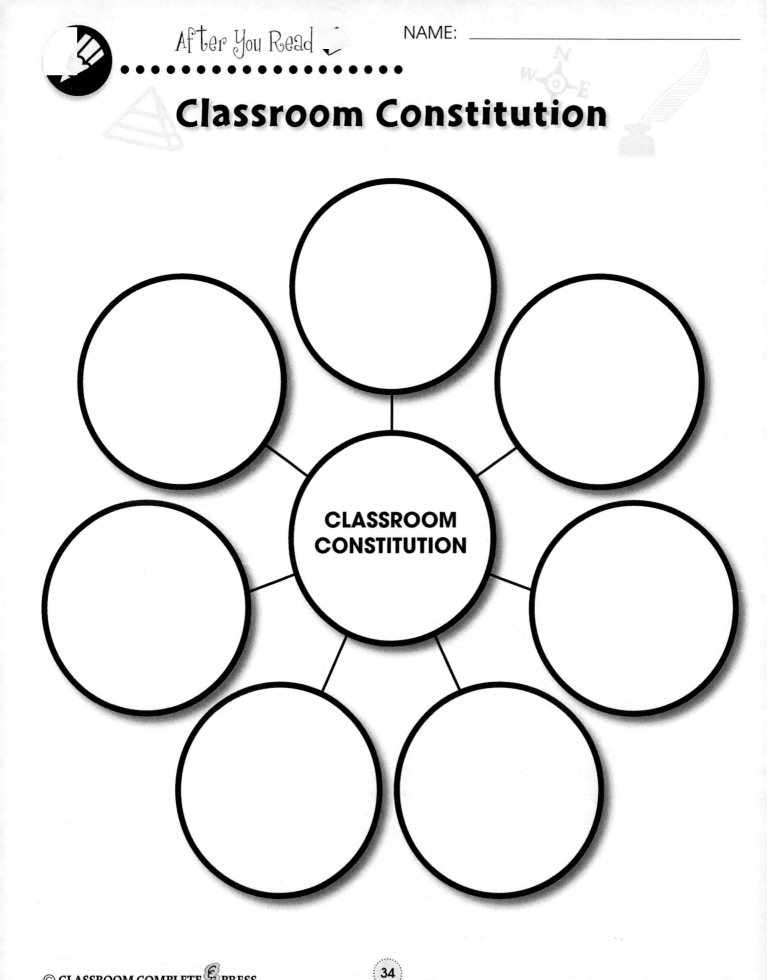

CLASSROOM CONSTITUTION

American Civil War CC5500

Crossword Puzzle!

Across

1. Eager to do something

3. Influence or effect

5. The idea of wanting to end something, especially slavery

7. Having a high order of importance

8. To give something up

11. System or structure

12. Decision or promise to do something

15. To formally withdraw

16. Separated into parts

Down

2. Person who shares the same feelings or concerns

4. To be worn out completely

6. To introduce industry to an area

9. Ability to deal skillfully

10. Believe in the powers and abilities of someone

13. Lowly and sometimes degrading

14. Forgiveness of an offence

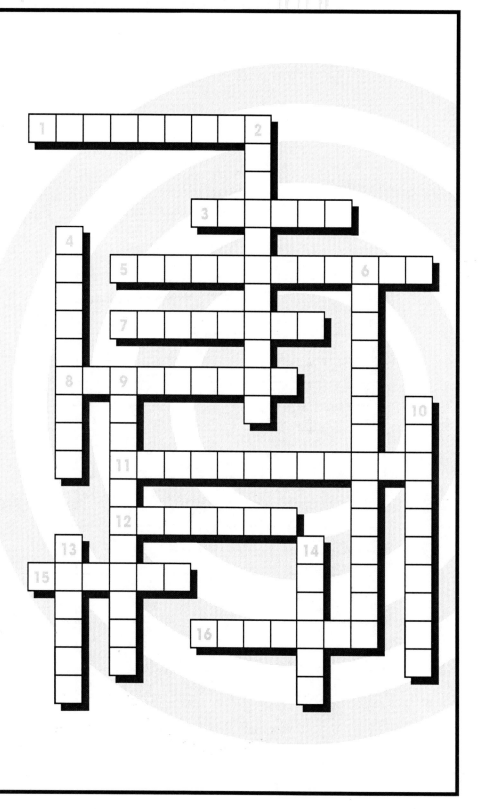

NAME: _____

Word Search

Find all of the words in the Word Search. Words are written horizontally, vertically, diagonally, and some are even written backwards.

AMENDMENTS	ANTEBELLUM	ASSASSINATED	CASUALTIES
BARRICADED	BANKRUPTCY	CONSTITUTION	CONTROVERSIAL
DEDICATION	HOMESICK	ECONOMY	DISCRIMINATION
ILLEGAL	INDEPENDENT	LEGITIMATE	OVERTHROW
MATERIALIZED	MANUFACTURING	PLANTATION	SEGREGATED
SUPERSEDE	WATERSHED	UNDISTINGUISHED	UNCONDITIONALLY

L	A	G	B	C	D	E	F	G	F	D	I	D	D	M	L	U	I
S	A	N	A	B	F	G	K	L	M	E	N	E	O	E	P	N	N
T	Z	I	I	J	K	L	M	N	O	D	T	D	G	Q	R	D	D
N	S	R	S	M	A	T	E	R	I	A	L	I	Z	E	D	I	E
E	D	U	T	R	X	Y	Z	G	N	C	T	C	D	F	O	S	P
M	E	T	P	S	E	T	U	I	V	I	W	A	X	Y	V	T	E
D	H	C	A	E	B	V	S	C	M	R	D	T	E	F	E	I	N
N	S	A	O	A	R	S	O	A	Z	R	E	I	F	G	R	N	D
E	R	F	B	N	A	S	T	R	E	A	E	O	G	U	T	G	E
M	E	U	C	S	O	E	E	G	T	B	H	N	N	I	H	U	N
A	T	N	S	O	K	M	L	D	M	N	O	C	P	Q	R	I	T
R	A	A	S	T	N	U	Y	W	E	S	O	Y	Z	A	O	S	B
C	W	M	D	E	F	S	G	H	I	N	J	C	K	L	W	H	M
Y	A	C	E	F	G	H	T	I	D	K	M	N	O	P	Q	E	R
I	C	N	O	I	T	A	N	I	M	I	R	C	S	I	D	D	Q
L	S	T	V	X	T	G	T	H	T	I	J	K	L	M	N	A	X
L	M	N	P	Q	R	I	C	A	S	U	A	L	T	I	E	S	T
E	C	D	E	U	O	G	H	N	O	I	T	A	T	N	A	L	P
G	A	B	A	N	R	B	H	O	M	E	S	I	C	K	Q	S	T
A	G	F	A	B	C	K	D	E	F	G	H	I	O	K	L	M	N
L	A	L	D	E	F	G	N	H	I	J	K	L	M	N	O	P	Q
A	L	C	D	E	D	E	T	A	G	E	R	G	E	S	G	H	K
Y	A	V	W	X	A	N	T	E	B	E	L	L	U	M	Q	X	G

After You Read

Comprehension Quiz

Part A   30   8

Circle the word True if the statement is true. Circle the word False if it is false.

1) The American Civil War took place between 1861 and 1865.
   True   **False**
2) The two sides in the war were the north and the south.
   True   **False**
3) One of the big issues in the war was slavery.
   True   **False**
4) Jefferson Davis was the U.S. President during the Civil War.
   True   **False**
5) When Fort Sumter was fired on, the Civil War began.
   True   **False**
6) The Battle of Fredericksburg is referred to as the "turning point".
   True   **False**
7) Black soldiers played a vital role in the Civil War.
   True   **False**
8) After the war there were no changes to the constitution.
   True   **False**

Part B   Fill in the blanks with the words provided. There will be six words left over.   10

abolish	Ulysses S. Grant	Gettysburg Address	Vicksburg
seceded	Emancipation Proclamation	Abraham Lincoln	depended
controversial	battles	Jefferson Davis	Gettysburg
surrendered	assassinated	Manassas	won

The American Civil War began after some southern states _____. People in the north
a
wanted to _____ slavery, but people in the south _____ on it. In 1861, Fort Sumter
b   c
was fired on and the Civil War began. In 1863 President _____ issued the _____.
d   e
This was very _____. There were many _____ in the Civil War. The Battle of
f   g
_____ has been called the "turning point" of the war. The Civil War ended when
h
General Lee _____ at the Appomattox Court House in 1865. The President had plans to
i
reconstruct the south, but many of his ideas did not succeed because he was _____.
j
The Civil War caused many changes in the United States. Even today, the Civil War is
considered one of the most important events in American history.

SUBTOTAL: /18

Comprehension Quiz

Part C

Answer the questions in complete sentences.

1. What were the **three major issues** in the American Civil War?

_____

_____

_____

2. Choose **one** of the battles discussed in this unit and describe what happened in that battle.

_____

_____

_____

3. Explain **at least two** ways the north and the south were **different** from each other.

_____

_____

_____

_____

4. What does it mean to **secede**?

_____

_____

5. What were **two** of the **major outcomes** of the Civil War?

_____

_____

_____

SUBTOTAL: **/12**

EZ✓

1.
a) illegal
b) valid
c) seceded
d) depended
e) sections
f) industrialized
g) resentment
h) abolitionism
i) opposed
j) economy
k) supersede
l) legitimate

2. Answers will vary

(7)

Accept any reasonable answers

(8)

1.
a) **True**
b) **False**
c) **False**
d) **True**
e) **True**
f) **False**
g) **True**
h) **False**

2.
a) seceded
b) opposed
c) valid
d) legitimate
e) illegal
f) abolitionism
g) economy
h) industrialized
i) depended
j) resentment
k) sections
l) supersede

(9)

1.
Possible answer: Slaves worked on farms and plantations which were the main industries in the south

4. **North:** industrialized, more immigrants, abolitionists
South: smaller population, agriculture

5. Answers will vary

6. Answers will vary

7. Answers will vary based on resource used

8. Answers will vary based on resource used

(10)

1.
undistinguished – **E**
ambitious – **G**
surrender – **A**
assassinated – **J**
regiment – **C**
bankruptcy – **L**
memoirs – **K**
demerit – **I**
plantation – **H**
martyr – **D**
pardon – **F**
quash – **B**

2. Answers will vary

3. Answers will vary

(11)

Answers will vary

(13)

1.
a) B
b) A
c) E
d) B
e) C
f) D

(14)

---

2. Answers will vary

3. Answers will vary

4. Answers will vary

5. Answers will vary based on resource used

6. Answers will vary

(15)

4.

Accept any answers that can be verified

5.

Redefined – Prefix: RE, Suffix: ED, Root: DEFINE

Malnourished – Prefix: MAL, SUFFIX: ED, Root: NOURISH

Unconditionally – Prefix: UN, Suffix: ALLY, Root: CONDITION

6.

Answers will vary

7.

Answers will vary based on resource used

8.

Answers will vary based on resource used

---

a) 11
b) 2
c) 7
d) 3
e) 9
f) 1
g) 14
h) 12
i) 4
j) 10
k) 15
l) 6
m) 8
n) 5
o) 13

2.

Answers will vary

3.

Answers will vary

---

a) private
b) retreated
c) barricaded
d) malnourished
e) priority
f) casualties
g) redefined
h) surrendered
i) exhausted
j) unconditionally
k) cofidence
l) dedication

2.

Answers will vary

Answers will vary

Answers will vary

---

a) sympathizers
b) equality
c) controversial
d) divided
e) independent
f) materialized
g) determined
h) resolve
i) overthrow

4.

Answers will vary based on resources used

One of the last major events of the Civil War – **F**

President Lincoln – **C**

Britain and France – **E**

Many people – **J**

The seceded states – **B**

Fort Sumter – **I**

President Lincoln – **D**

The Emancipation Proclamation – **A**

An executive order – **G**

The attack on Fort Sumter – **H**

2.

Answers will vary

---

divided – **C**

materialized – **E**

determined – **F**

independent – **G**

sympathizer – **A**

controversial – **I**

overthrow – **H**

resolve – **D**

equality – **B**

2.

Answers will vary

3.

Answers will vary

4.

Answers will vary

2.

a) watershed

b) reconstruct

c) constitution
d) amendments
e) critical
f) slavery
g) legal
h) dramatically

3. Possible answers: Amendments to the constitution (13th, 14th, 15th), end of slavery, assassination of Lincoln

4. Answers will vary

5. Answers will vary

6. Constitutional amendments still affect people's lives today

---

1.

a) B

b) C

c) D

d) A

e) C

f) B

1.

slavery – **E**

constitution – **H**

reconstruct – **J**

federal – **G**

goals – **A**

antebellum – **B**

amendments – **F**

dramatically – **K**

applied – **L**

watershed – **C**

legal – **D**

critical – **I**

2. Answers will vary

3. Answers will vary

Answers will vary

5.

a) impact

b) organization
c) homesick
d) resourceful

e) strategies

f) discrimination
g) segregated
h) menial

i) manufacturing

6. Answers will vary based on resource used

7. Answers will vary

1.

a) **True**

b) **False**

c) **False**

d) **True**

e) **True**

f) **True**

g) **False**

h) **True**

i) **False**

j) **True**

2. Answers will vary

3. Answers will vary

4. Answers will vary

1.

a) impact

b) menial

c) discrimination

d) resourceful

e) homesick

f) segregated

g) strategies

h) organization

i) manufacturing

2. Answers will vary

3. Answers will vary

4. Answers will vary

Answers will vary

Word Search Answers

Across
1. ambitious
3. impact
5. abolitionism
7. priority
8. surrender
11. organization
12. resolve
15. secede
16. divided

Down
2. sympathizer
4. exhausted
6. industrialized
9. resourceful
10. confidence
13. menial
14. pardon

Part A
1) True
2) True
3) True
4) False
5) True
6) False
7) True
8) False

Part B
a) seceded
b) abolish
c) depended
d) Abraham Lincoln
e) Emancipation Proclamation
f) controversial
g) battles
h) Gettysburg
i) surrendered
j) assassinated

Part C

1. Slavery, North vs. South (industry, agriculture), States' rights

2. Answers will vary

3. Possible answers:
North: higher population, abolitionists, more immigrants, more representation in government.
South: lower population, slavery used on farms and plantations, some states seceded, felt powerless with fewer representatives in government

4. to break away

5. Possible answers: No states ever seceded again, change in constitution with 13th, 14th and 15th amendments

American Civil War CC5500

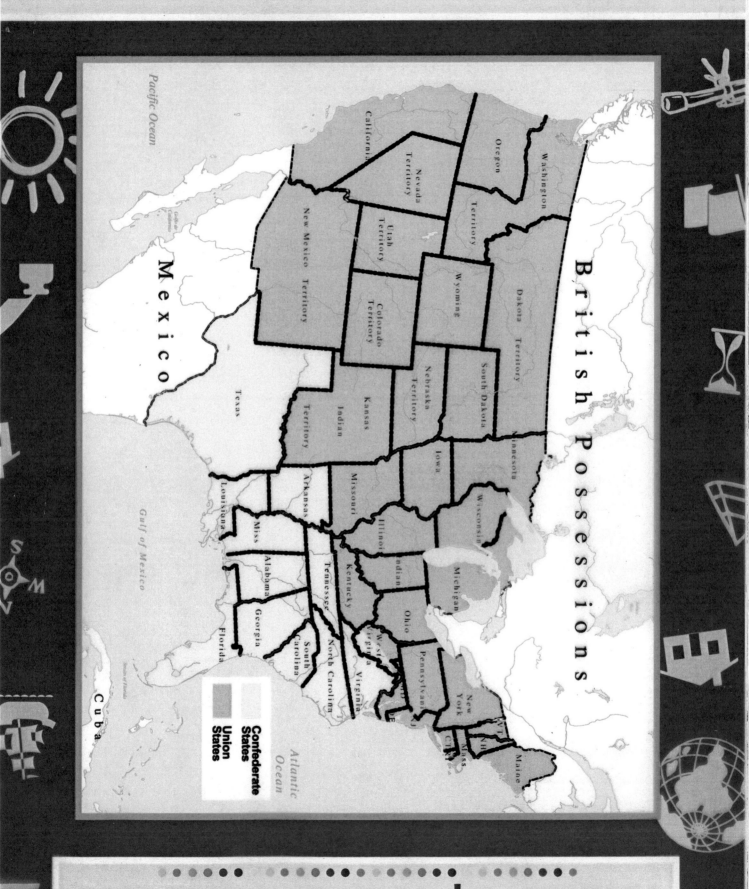

Political Map of America 1861-1865

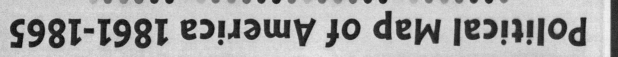

Lincoln's Gettysburg Address
(November 19th 1863)

"Fourscore and seven years ago our fathers brought forth, on this continent, a new nation, conceived in liberty, and dedicated to the proposition that all men are created equal. Now we are engaged in a great civil war, testing whether that nation, or any nation so conceived, and so dedicated, can long endure. We are met on a great battle-field of that war. We have come to dedicate a portion of that field, as a final resting-place for those who here gave their lives, that that nation might live. It is altogether fitting and proper that we should do this. But, in a larger sense, we cannot dedicate, we cannot consecrate—we cannot hallow—this ground. The brave men, living and dead, who struggled here, have consecrated it far above our poor power to add or detract. The world will little note, nor long remember what we say here, but it can never forget what they did here. It is for us the living, rather, to be dedicated here to the unfinished work which they who fought here have thus far so nobly advanced. It is rather for us to be here dedicated to the great task remaining before us—that from these honored dead we take increased devotion to that cause for which they here gave the last full measure of devotion—that we here highly resolve that these dead shall not have died in vain—that this nation, under God, shall have a new birth of freedom, and that government of the people, by the people, for the people, shall not perish from the earth."

Land Lost To Confederacy

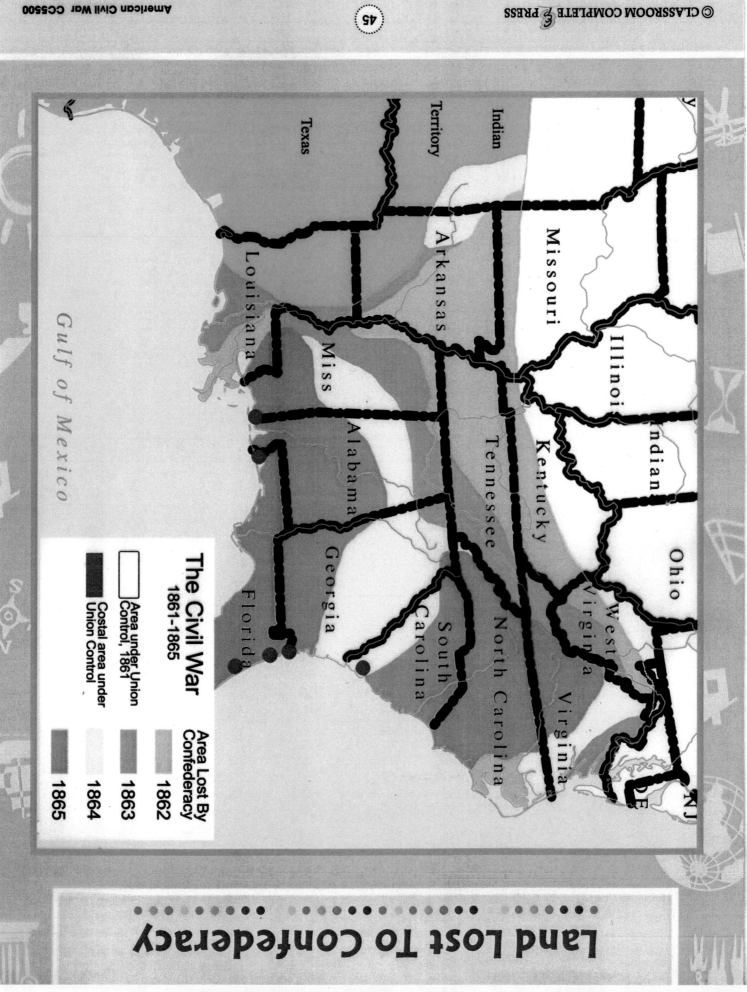

The Civil War
1861-1865

Area under Union Control, 1861

Costal area under Union Control

Area Lost By Confederacy

- 1862
- 1863
- 1864
- 1865

Gulf of Mexico

Texas

Territory

Indian

Arkansas

Missouri

Louisiana

Illinois

Indian

Miss

Alabama

Tennessee

Kentucky

Ohio

Georgia

Florida

South Carolina

North Carolina

West Virginia

Virginia

NJ

Fort Sumter SC
(Attacked on April 1861 which started the war)

Edwin Stanton

Gettysburg Lincoln Speech

Judah P. Benjamin

Alexander Stephens

Civil War Monuments, Statues & Memorials

Civil War Monument

Gettysburg National Cemetery

Lincoln Statue

Publication Listing

• • • • • • • • • • • • • • • •

Ask Your Dealer About Our Complete Line

ENVIRONMENTAL STUDIES

ITEM #	TITLE
	MANAGING OUR WASTE SERIES
CC5764	Waste: At the Source
CC5765	Prevention, Recycling & Conservation
CC5766	Waste: The Global View
CC5767	Waste Management Big Book
	CLIMATE CHANGE SERIES
CC5769	Global Warming: Causes
CC5770	Global Warming: Effects
CC5771	Global Warming: Reduction
CC5772	Global Warming Big Book
	GLOBAL WATER SERIES
CC5773	Conservation: Fresh Water Resources
CC5774	Conservation: Ocean Water Resources
CC5775	Conservation: Waterway Habitats Resources
CC5776	Water Conservation Big Book
	CARBON FOOTPRINT SERIES
CC5778	Reducing Your Own Carbon Footprint
CC5779	Reducing Your School's Carbon Footprint
CC5780	Reducing Your Community's Carbon Footprint
CC5781	Carbon Footprint Big Book

LANGUAGE ARTS

ITEM #	TITLE
	WRITING SKILLS SERIES
CC1100	How to Write a Paragraph
CC1101	How to Write a Book Report
CC1102	How to Write an Essay
CC1103	Master Writing Big Book
	READING SKILLS SERIES
CC1116	Reading Comprehension
CC1117	Literary Devices
CC1118	Critical Thinking
CC1119	Master Reading Big Book

REGULAR & REMEDIAL EDUCATION

• • • • • • • • • • • • • •

Reading Level 3-4 Grades 5-8

SCIENCE

ITEM #	TITLE
	ECOLOGY & THE ENVIRONMENT SERIES
CC4500	Ecosystems
CC4501	Classification & Adaptation
CC4502	Cells
CC4503	Ecology & The Environment Big Book
	MATTER & ENERGY SERIES
CC4504	Properties of Matter
CC4505	Atoms, Molecules & Elements
CC4506	Energy
CC4507	The Nature of Matter Big Book
	FORCE & MOTION SERIES
CC4508	Force
CC4509	Motion
CC4510	Simple Machines
CC4511	Force, Motion & Simple Machines Big Book
	SPACE & BEYOND SERIES
CC4512	Space - Solar Systems
CC4513	Space - Galaxies & The Universe
CC4514	Space - Travel & Technology
CC4515	Space Big Book
	HUMAN BODY SERIES
CC4516	Cells, Skeletal & Muscular Systems
CC4517	Nervous, Senses & Respiratory Systems
CC4518	Circulatory, Digestive & Reproductive Systems
CC4519	Human Body Big Book

SOCIAL STUDIES

ITEM #	TITLE
	NORTH AMERICAN GOVERNMENTS SERIES
CC5757	American Government
CC5758	Canadian Government
CC5759	Mexican Government
CC5760	Governments of North America Big Book
	WORLD GOVERNMENTS SERIES
CC5761	World Political Leaders
CC5762	World Electoral Processes
CC5763	Capitalism vs. Communism
CC5777	World Politics Big Book
	WORLD CONFLICT SERIES
CC5500	American Civil War
CC5511	American Revolutionary War
CC5512	American Wars Big Book
CC5501	World War I
CC5502	World War II
CC5503	World Wars I & II Big Book
CC5505	Korean War
CC5506	Vietnam War
CC5507	Korean & Vietnam Wars Big Book
CC5508	Persian Gulf War (1990-1991)
CC5509	Iraq War (2003-2010)
CC5510	Gulf Wars Big Book
	WORLD CONTINENTS SERIES
CC5750	North America
CC5751	South America
CC5768	The Americas Big Book
CC5752	Europe
CC5753	Africa
CC5754	Asia
CC5755	Australia
CC5756	Antarctica
	WORLD CONNECTIONS SERIES
CC5782	Culture, Society & Globalization
CC5783	Economy & Globalization
CC5784	Technology & Globalization
CC5785	Globalization Big Book
	MAPPING SKILLS SERIES
CC5786	Grades PK-2 Mapping Skills with Google Earth
CC5787	Grades 3-5 Mapping Skills with Google Earth
CC5788	Grades 6-8 Mapping Skills with Google Earth
CC5789	Grades PK-8 Mapping Skills with Google Earth Big Book

VISIT:

www.CLASSROOM COMPLETE PRESS.com

To view sample pages from each book

LITERATURE KITS™

ITEM #	TITLE
	GRADES 1-2
CC2100	Curious George (H. A. Rey)
CC2101	Paper Bag Princess (Robert N. Munsch)
CC2102	Stone Soup (Marcia Brown)
CC2103	The Very Hungry Caterpillar (Eric Carle)
CC2104	Where the Wild Things Are (Maurice Sendak)
	GRADES 3-4
CC2300	Babe: The Gallant Pig (Dick King-Smith)
CC2301	Because of Winn-Dixie (Kate DiCamillo)
CC2302	The Tale of Despereaux (Kate DiCamillo)
CC2303	James and the Giant Peach (Roald Dahl)
CC2304	Ramona Quimby, Age 8 (Beverly Cleary)
CC2305	The Mouse and the Motorcycle (Beverly Cleary)
CC2306	Charlotte's Web (E.B. White)
CC2307	Owls in the Family (Farley Mowat)
CC2308	Sarah, Plain and Tall (Patricia MacLachlan)
CC2309	Matilda (Roald Dahl)
CC2310	Charlie & The Chocolate Factory (Roald Dahl)
CC2311	Frindle (Andrew Clements)
CC2312	M.C. Higgins, the Great (Virginia Hamilton)
CC2313	The Family Under The Bridge (N.S. Carlson)
	GRADES 5-6
CC2500	Black Beauty (Anna Sewell)
CC2501	Bridge to Terabithia (Katherine Paterson)
CC2502	Bud, Not Buddy (Christopher Paul Curtis)
CC2503	The Egypt Game (Zilpha Keatley Snyder)
CC2504	The Great Gilly Hopkins (Katherine Paterson)
CC2505	Holes (Louis Sachar)
CC2506	Number the Stars (Lois Lowry)
CC2507	The Sign of the Beaver (E.G. Speare)
CC2508	The Whipping Boy (Sid Fleischman)
CC2509	Island of the Blue Dolphins (Scott O'Dell)
CC2510	Underground to Canada (Barbara Smucker)
CC2511	Loser (Jerry Spinelli)
CC2512	The Higher Power of Lucky (Susan Patron)
CC2513	Kira-Kira (Cynthia Kadohata)
CC2514	Dear Mr. Henshaw (Beverly Cleary)
CC2515	The Summer of the Swans (Betsy Byars)
CC2516	Shiloh (Phyllis Reynolds Naylor)
CC2517	A Single Shard (Linda Sue Park)
CC2518	Hoot (Carl Hiaasen)
CC2519	Hatchet (Gary Paulsen)
CC2520	The Giver (Lois Lowry)
CC2521	The Graveyard Book (Neil Gaiman)
	GRADES 7-8
CC2700	Cheaper by the Dozen (Frank B. Gilbreth)
CC2701	The Miracle Worker (William Gibson)
CC2702	The Red Pony (John Steinbeck)
CC2703	Treasure Island (Robert Louis Stevenson)
CC2704	Romeo & Juliet (William Shakespeare)
CC2705	Crispin: The Cross of Lead (Avi)

REGULAR EDUCATION

LANGUAGE ARTS

ITEM #	TITLE
	READING RESPONSE FORMS SERIES
CC1106	Reading Response Forms: Grades 1-2
CC1107	Reading Response Forms: Grades 3-4
CC1108	Reading Response Forms: Grades 5-6
CC1109	Reading Response Forms Big Book: Grades 1-6
	WORD FAMILIES SERIES
CC1110	Word Families - Short Vowels: Grades PK-1
CC1111	Word Families - Long Vowels: Grades PK-1
CC1112	Word Families - Vowels Big Book: Grades K-1
	SIGHT & PICTURE WORDS SERIES
CC1113	High Frequency Sight Words: Grades PK-1
CC1114	High Frequency Picture Words: Grades PK-1
CC1115	Sight & Picture Words Big Book Grades PK-1

INTERACTIVE WHITEBOARD SOFTWARE

ITEM #	TITLE
	CLIMATE CHANGE SERIES
CC7747	Global Warming: Causes Grades 3-8
CC7748	Global Warming: Effects Grades 3-8
CC7749	Global Warming: Reduction Grades 3-8
CC7750	Global Warming Big Box Grades 3-8
	HUMAN BODY SERIES
CC7549	Cells, Skeletal & Muscular Systems Grades 3-8
CC7550	Senses, Nervous & Respiratory Systems Grades 3-8
CC7551	Circulatory, Digestive & Reproductive Systems Grades 3-8
CC7552	Human Body Big Box Grades 3-8
	FORCE, MOTION & SIMPLE MACHINES SERIES
CC7553	Force Grades 3-8
CC7554	Motion Grades 3-8
CC7555	Simple Machines Grades 3-8
CC7556	Force, Motion & Simple Machines Big Box Grades 3-8
	WRITING SKILLS SERIES
CC7104	How to Write a Paragraph Grades 3-8
CC7105	How to Write a Book Report Grades 3-8
CC7106	How to Write an Essay Grades 3-8
CC7107	Master Writing Big Box Grades 3-8
	READING SKILLS SERIES
CC7108	Reading Comprehension Grades 3-8
CC7109	Literary Devices Grades 3-8
CC7110	Critical Thinking Grades 3-8
CC7111	Master Reading Big Box Grades 3-8
	SIGHT & PICTURE WORDS SERIES
CC7100	High Frequency Sight Words Grades PK-2
CC7101	High Frequency Picture Words Grades PK-2
CC7102	Sight & Picture Words Big Box Grades PK-2

MATHEMATICS

ITEM #	TITLE
	PRINCIPLES & STANDARDS OF MATH SERIES
CC3100	Grades PK-2 Number & Operations Task Sheets
CC3101	Grades PK-2 Algebra Task Sheets
CC3102	Grades PK-2 Geometry Task Sheets
CC3103	Grades PK-2 Measurement Task Sheets
CC3104	Grades PK-2 Data Analysis & Probability Task Sheets
CC3105	Grades PK-2 Five Strands of Math Big Book Task Sheets
CC3106	Grades 3-5 Number & Operations Task Sheets
CC3107	Grades 3-5 Algebra Task Sheets
CC3108	Grades 3-5 Geometry Task Sheets
CC3109	Grades 3-5 Measurement Task Sheets
CC3110	Grades 3-5 Data Analysis & Probability Task Sheets
CC3111	Grades 3-5 Five Strands of Math Big Book Task Sheets
CC3112	Grades 6-8 Number & Operations Task Sheets
CC3113	Grades 6-8 Algebra Task Sheets
CC3114	Grades 6-8 Geometry Task Sheets
CC3115	Grades 6-8 Measurement Task Sheets
CC3116	Grades 6-8 Data Analysis & Probability Task Sheets
CC3117	Grades 6-8 Five Strands of Math Big Book Task Sheets
	PRINCIPLES & STANDARDS OF MATH SERIES
CC3200	Grades PK-2 Number & Operations Drill Sheets
CC3201	Grades PK-2 Algebra Drill Sheets
CC3202	Grades PK-2 Geometry Drill Sheets
CC3203	Grades PK-2 Measurement Drill Sheets
CC3204	Grades PK-2 Data Analysis & Probability Drill Sheets
CC3205	Grades PK-2 Five Strands of Math Big Book Drill Sheets
CC3206	Grades 3-5 Number & Operations Drill Sheets
CC3207	Grades 3-5 Algebra Drill Sheets
CC3208	Grades 3-5 Geometry Drill Sheets
CC3209	Grades 3-5 Measurement Drill Sheets
CC3210	Grades 3-5 Data Analysis & Probability Drill Sheets
CC3211	Grades 3-5 Five Strands of Math Big Book Drill Sheets
CC3212	Grades 6-8 Number & Operations Drill Sheets
CC3213	Grades 6-8 Algebra Drill Sheets
CC3214	Grades 6-8 Geometry Drill Sheets
CC3215	Grades 6-8 Measurement Drill Sheets
CC3216	Grades 6-8 Data Analysis & Probability Drill Sheets
CC3217	Grades 6-8 Five Strands of Math Big Book Drill Sheets
	PRINCIPLES & STANDARDS OF MATH SERIES
CC3300	Grades PK-2 Number & Operations Task & Drill Sheets
CC3301	Grades PK-2 Algebra Task & Drill Sheets
CC3302	Grades PK-2 Geometry Task & Drill Sheets
CC3303	Grades PK-2 Measurement Task & Drill Sheets
CC3304	Grades PK-2 Data Analysis & Probability Task & Drill
CC3306	Grades 3-5 Number & Operations Task & Drill Sheets
CC3307	Grades 3-5 Algebra Task & Drill Sheets
CC3308	Grades 3-5 Geometry Task & Drill Sheets
CC3309	Grades 3-5 Measurement Task & Drill Sheets
CC3310	Grades 3-5 Data Analysis & Probability Task & Drill
CC3312	Grades 6-8 Number & Operations Task & Drill Sheets
CC3313	Grades 6-8 Algebra Task & Drill Sheets
CC3314	Grades 6-8 Geometry Task & Drill Sheets
CC3315	Grades 6-8 Measurement Task & Drill Sheets
CC3316	Grades 6-8 Data Analysis & Probability Task & Drill